MW01041257

PowerPhonics™

Be Safe on the Bus

Learning the B Sound

Kathy Smith

The Rosen Publishing Group's
PowerKids Press™
New York

Be a safe bus rider.

Stand back while you wait.

Watch out for cars and bikes.

Wait for the bus to stop before getting on.

SCHOOL BUS
GMC

Watch your step getting on the bus.

5184

Always wear your seat belt.

PRESS

Keep your hands inside the bus.

Sit down until the bus stops.

Walk off the bus.

Always walk in front of the bus.
Never walk behind the bus.

SCHOOL BUS
STOP
179

Word List

back

be

before

behind

belt

bikes

bus

Instructional Guide

Note to Instructors:
One of the essential skills that enable a young child to read is the ability to associate letter-sound symbols and blend these sounds to form words. Phonics instruction can teach children a system that will help them decode unfamiliar words and, in turn, enhance their word-recognition skills. We offer a phonics-based series of books that are easy to read and understand. Each book pairs words and pictures that reinforce specific phonetic sounds in a logical sequence. Topics are based on curriculum goals appropriate for early readers in the areas of science, social studies, and health.

Letter/Sound: **b** – Have the child cut out pictures of objects whose names begin with **b** from magazines and catalogs. Have them mount the cutouts on a banner labeled "Big Banner of B Words." Label the banner items. Make matching word cards. Have the child match the word cards to the words on the banner.

Phonics Activities: Assist the child with making a collage of pictures whose names start with **b** and paste them on a poster. Ask the child to write the names of the **b** pictures on an attached piece of paper and read these words to you.

- Ask the child to name the beginning consonant **b** word that means the opposite of *little (big)*. Continue with: *girl (boy), front (back), good (bad), ugly (beautiful), sell (buy)*. List answers on a chalkboard or dry-erase board, and have the child underline the initial **b** in each of them.
- Prepare a bingo game by writing the following letters on a bingo card: **m**, **t**, **p**, **short a**, and **b**. Show pictures of an item that starts with one of the above sounds. Have the child use bingo markers to cover the given letter-sound on the bingo card. Continue until the child has bingo. As a variation, prepare cards with words instead of letters. Write words on the chalkboard or dry-erase board, and have the child find the matching words on the bingo card.

Additional Resources:

- Feldman, Heather L. *My School Bus: A Book about School Bus Safety*. New York: The Rosen Publishing Group, Inc., 1998.
- Mattern, Joanne. *Safety at School*. Minneapolis, MN: ABDO Publishing Company, 1999.
- Raatma, Lucia. *Safety on the School Bus*. Mankato, MN: Capstone, Press, Inc., 1999.

Published in 2002 by The Rosen Publishing Group, Inc.
29 East 21st Street, New York, NY 10010

Book Design: Ron A. Churley

Photo Credits: Cover © Charles Shoffner/Index Stock; pp. 3, 5 © SuperStock; p. 7 © Gary Buss/FPG International; p. 9 © Jeff Dunn/Index Stock; p. 11 © M. Siluk/The Image Works; p. 13 by Karey L. Schuckers-Churley; p. 15 © C. W. McKeen/The Image Works; p. 17 by Donna Scholl; p. 19 © Zephyr Picture/International Stock; p. 21 © Michael Schwarz/The Image Works.

Library of Congress Cataloging-in-Publication Data

Smith, Kathy, 1971-
Be safe on the bus: learning the B sound / Kathy Smith.
p. cm. — (Power phonics/phonics for the real world)
ISBN 0-8239-5900-7 (lib. bdg.)
ISBN 0-8239-8245-9 (pbk.)
6-pack ISBN 0-8239-9213-6
1. School children—Transportation—Safety measures—Juvenile literature. 2. School buses—Safety regulations—Juvenile literature. [1. School buses—Safety measures. 2. Safety.] I. Title. II. Series.

LB2864 .S62 2002
363.12'59—dc21

00-013033

Manufactured in the United States of America